Gathering

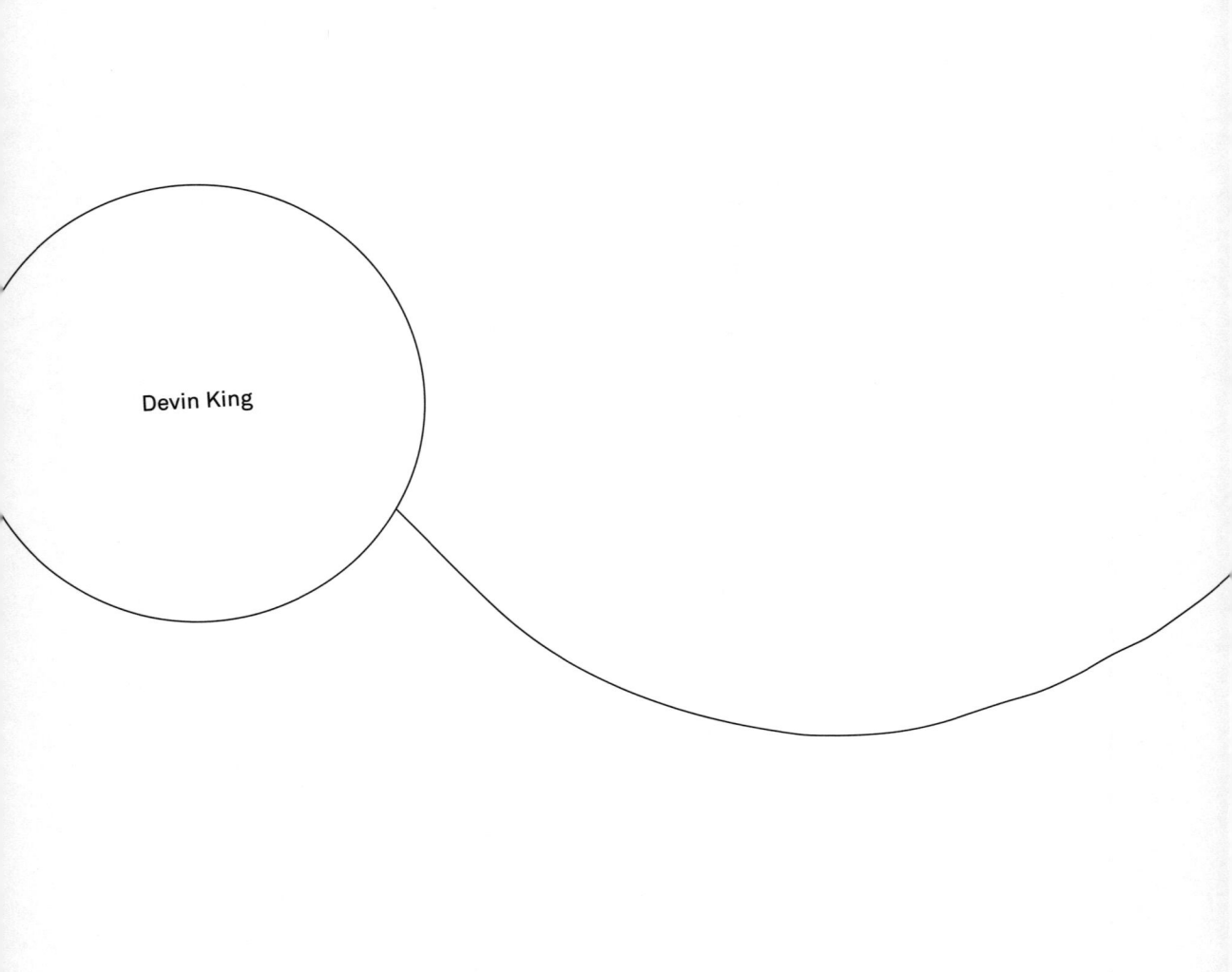

Devin King

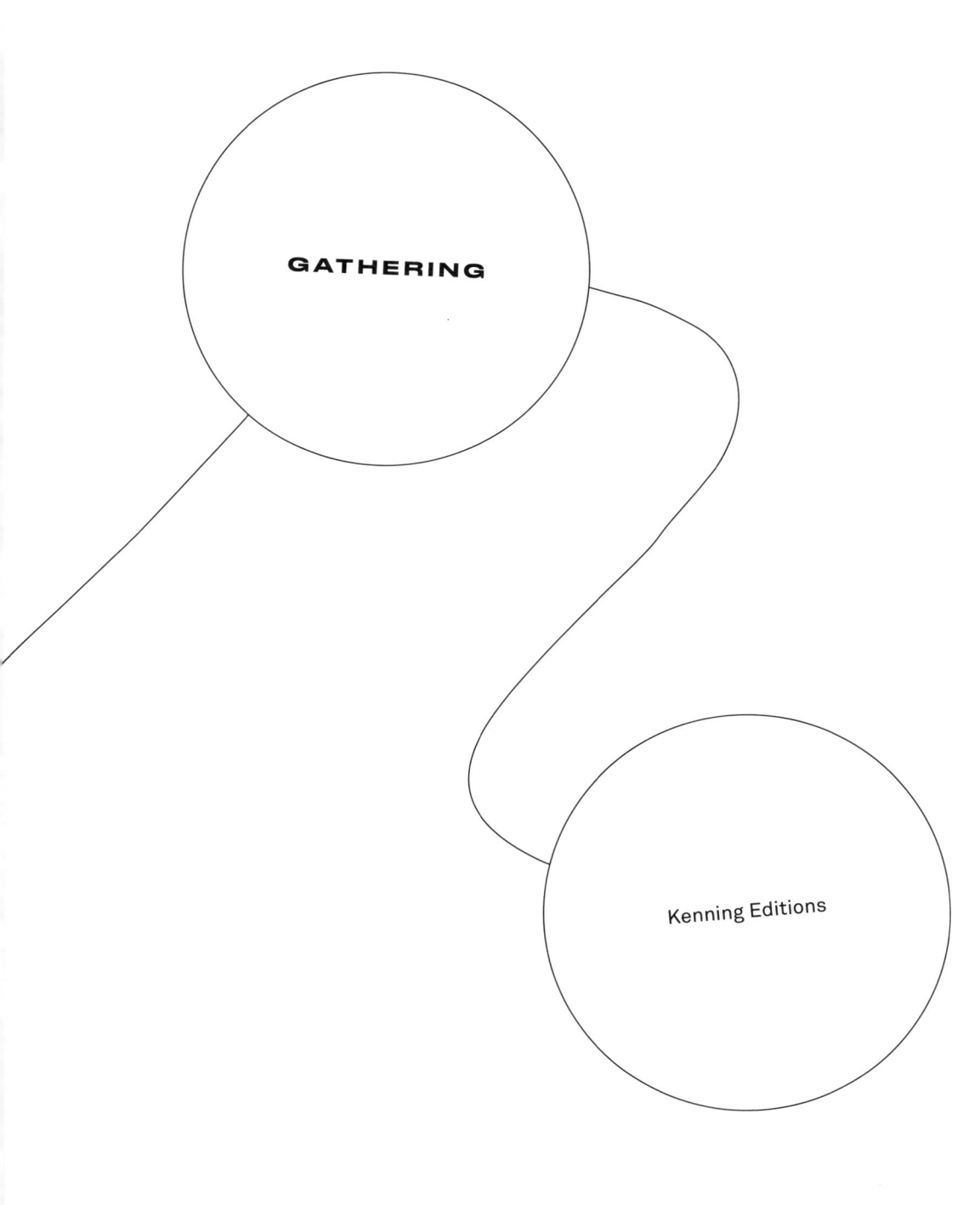

GATHERING

Kenning Editions

Copyright © 2023 by Devin King
Published in Chicago by Kenning Editions

kenningeditions.com

Distributed by Small Press Distribution
1341 Seventh St., Berkeley, CA 94710
spdbooks.org

ISBN 979-8-9856628-3-2
LCCN 2022950706

Designed by Crisis

Kenning Editions is a 501c3 non-profit,
independent literary publisher
investigating the relationships of
aesthetic quality to political commitment.
Consider donating or subscribing:
kenningeditions.com/shop/donation.

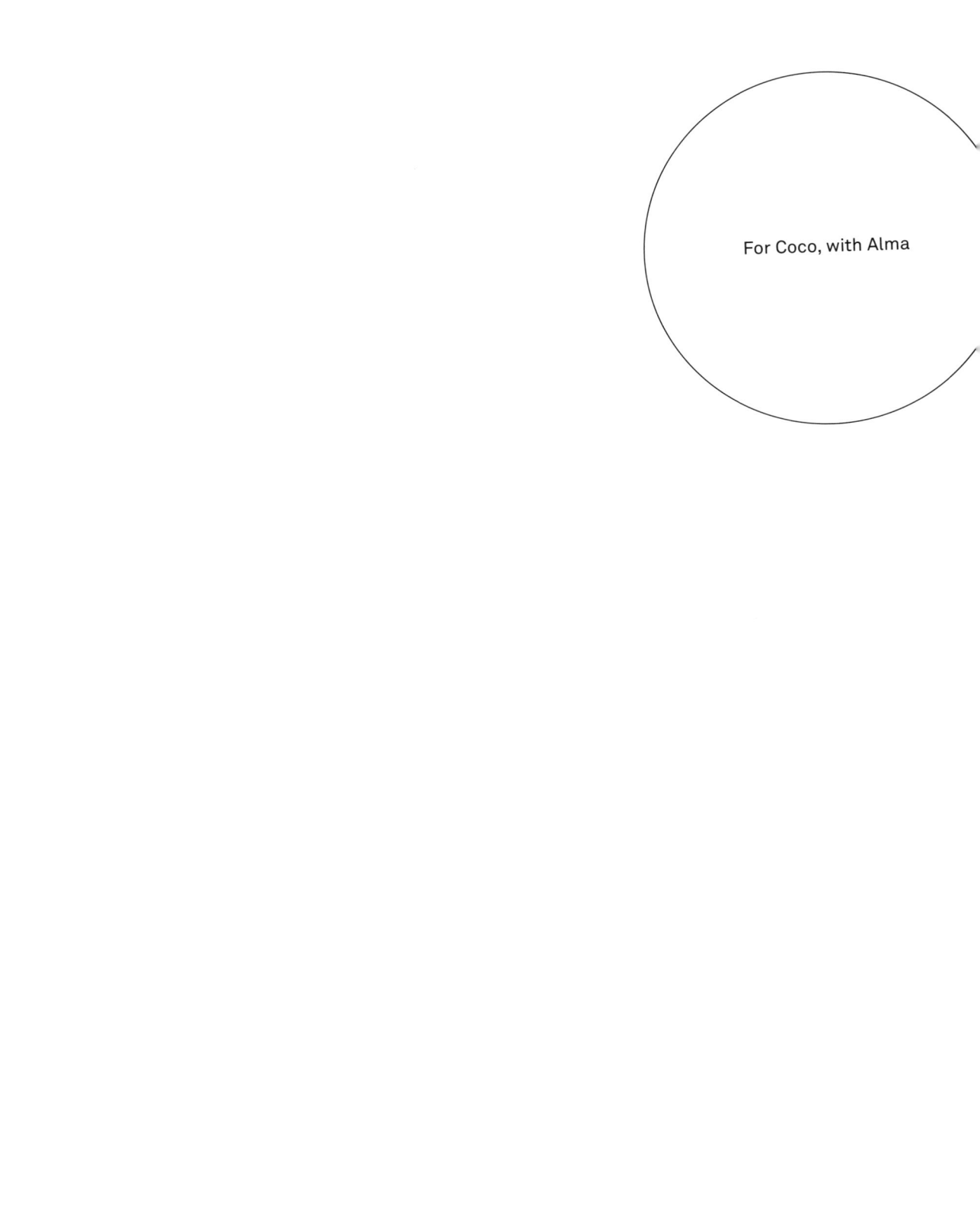

For Coco, with Alma

I think, I don't know if I could prove it, etc., that ultimately Ez' use of the "ideogrammic" extends nothing that isn't literally evident in Stendhal.
—Robert Creeley to Charles Olson, May 19, 1952

. . . such wondrous thoughts,—
such wondrous joys in the world
which would come from thinking!
—Anthony Trollope,
The Eustace Diamonds

1

1   Geoffrey's lift phfoomphs his girl's pastel dresses.
    "We know how to get to Clarice's," they say.
    "But you're going too fast for your mother."
    Katherine, behind them, with the baby.
    They walk past the vape store, Walgreens, the bar.

2   Across the street, boys loudly quote Trollope.
    "'My address will be The Bull, Willingford' . . .
    I'm so over people," Thom says, Kevin
    laughs, zips and unzips his shiny bomber,
    "No more novels. I'm switching to theory."

3   Clarice finds Parliament in the bookshelf,
    sends Colin with her upstairs to Xbox.
    See Clarice form and plate beet bruschetta.
    Noa appears dressed, puts on Emmylou.
    "What can I do?" "Put these out. Make a drink."

4   Clarice and Noa had evenings.
    People went to their home and stood and talked
    near the stairs or on the well-dyed carpet
    about where they lived now and what they might make
    and what they might buy and how often they thought
    of quitting the things they all must have tried.
    The justification of compromise,
    the production of consequential fact,
    the gift of regulated emotion.

5   Martin and Tully—shop-owners—arrive.
Colin receives their impolite children.
"At least they're boys," he thinks, "we'll play FIFA."
His manners matched downstairs by his parents.
"Caught a knucklehead trying to shoplift."

6   The crypto-racism is marked, ignored;
long friendship is a kind of magic trick
learned in secret, master and apprentice
both performed by the mind that plays wizard
in solitude and rebel to itself.

7   "There's two more," Noa says, shoving large drinks
into Martin's and Tully's larger hands.
"Sorry, we've got a thing later," Brian says.
"We'll probably leave before dessert."
He playfully punches Noa's kidneys.

8   Kim, his wife, floats above the attractive
chair, accepts the heavy whiskey. The room
watches her drink—POUNCE!—Noa grabs the cat
as the liquor roosts everywhere but her.
"Colin!" "Whu-ut?!" "Come get your cat!" "Da-ad!"

9   "I'm so sorry." "It's no problem, nothing
got on my dress—just let me wash my hands."
Noa hands Colin Parliament, Clarice
hands Noa a sponge. Martin and Tully
watch Brian and Clarice in the kitchen.

10   "Can I help chop?" said Brian, eating nuts.
"No, no, everything's close. I'm just stirring."
He set his wine too hard on the island.
"I read that Montaigne essay you gave me.
I loved reading something Shakespeare read too."

11   Besides entrenched couples their age, the two
invited pass-throughs, a smattering of
younger friends—students of Clarice's or
boys, always boys, Noa found at readings.
Enter red-faced, smoke-auraed Trollope boys.

12   Already uncomfortable, the kids,
rather than asking to help, stand in need
of urgent rescue that never comes. So,
Kevin and Thom meet Dara and Zoë.
Youth with youth, age, age. Noise underlined talk.

13   Dara, underdressed and yoga-piquant
proposes friendship's asset: knowledge
of private aches. "Zoë's working on a play."
Thom: "Oh re-eally?" Kevin's more polite.
"I don't think I've ever met a playwright."

14   "Hasn't the theatergoing middle-class
turned to the telly?" said Thom. Kevin snorts.
Zoë gamely follows Thom's fake accent.
"The telly? Where the fuck are you from, mate?"
Dara tilts her glass back and chews on ice.

15   Geoffrey and the baby circle the room.
      He sips white wine between cooing handoffs
      and lets Katherine talk loudly with her friends.
      "I can read while I nurse, but it's so slow,
      I might as well just memorize Leibniz."

16   "It would help if you read the English, Kat."
      Clarice and Katherine know only laughter,
      their department otherwise a refuge
      for particular men in pleats without
      interest in niceties won by bodies.

17   They absorb Kevin fumbling in the fridge.
      "Can I help you with something?" Clarice says,
      winking at Katherine. Zoë, still flirting
      with Thom, watches Kevin make eye contact
      with the space between the older women.

18   "Is all this beer ok to drink?" "Of course."
      He chooses an oversized dark Belgian,
      unwraps the gold foil and pops the cork.
      "Do you want a glass?" "No, the bottle's fine."
      He sneezes as bubbles go up his nose.

19   Noa, buzzing for half an hour now
      tops off his drink and calls them all to sit.
      The table is simply set and well-stocked.
      There are benches and chairs from other rooms
      the guests settle in as the hosts disappear.

20   I can no longer remember the food
Clarice and Noa brought to the table,
but I do remember looking sideways
at Lily, my love, between plates, touching
her thigh in confidence as Deray spoke.

21   We were drawn to him, a group of seven
or so from both sides of the table, by
the round song of his voice, attendant
to more life than the night's easy chatter.
Geoffrey knew Deray and asked how he was.

22   "I'm acting again. That's a surprise. Bright
thoughts of my small creative beginnings
are inside me. If you don't mind, I'd love
an occasion like this one—small, polite,
but also public—to tell my story."

23   Our silence answered.
                        "I was a painter.
In my teens, it was all I could hope to
get a show at the coffee house. This was
before computers took over—instead
the unwashed in flannels read the Russians.

24   "I should say *a* Russian. Dostoevsky.
Or, if not, they were sketching in spiral
notebooks. That was me. A weird Black kid with
graphite fingers and americano
au-laits. My life was dear and off-kilter.

25 "I got my show. I got into art school.
And my painting instructor was the first
person to tell me I was wasting my time.
Couldn't I see I wasn't a painter?
But I kept on taking different classes.

26 "Like most younger artists I began enthralled
with my own figure and those of my friends.
What else do they show in coffee houses?
But as I progressed I needed something
different, denser, to concentrate on.

27 "I knew so many people then I would
barely bother with now. My roommate Claire—
this was someone I spent all my time with—
would get me drunk and drag me to things I
never cared for. She drove me crazy too.

28 "Free champagne. We vogued along the upper
balcony of the opera house, laughing,
making fun of other people to feel
less out of place in our shabby-chic clothes.
We heard the chimes and went to find our seats.

29 "As the pre-show announcements began I
scanned the plush crowd for people to shit on.
On the aisle across, a few rows down,
I saw a man unbuttoning his shirt.
The lights dimmed. His right hand cupped his left breast.

30 "I pointed him out to Claire. She giggled.
    We held the power buttons on our phones.
    Please understand me, it is not the fact
    of this performance I want to convey,
    or that I acted as witness to it.

31 "I have spent most of my life in cities.
    I walk to get coffee in the morning
    and take buses to see about new things.
    So I am prepared for the critical
    mask this objective world holds out to me.

32 "I have taken it; I have worn it well,
    have learned how it feels when it touches skin.
    My father, professor soon to be dean,
    looks up from his laden desk to ask me:
    'Can remonstrance live in solitude?'

33 "In my painting I always emphasized
    borders, so that the flat reality
    my mind consumed in soft visitations
    my eyes flashed with transitional effort
    became a series of states in concert.

34 "But, suddenly, as the knight onstage took
    water from the bowl and sprinkled it on
    the rock, the orchestra signaling rain
    and the stage lights flashing weighted lightning,
    these borders, made by my eyes, became husks.

35   "These borders became dark husks of the mind—
their outlines vanished into dense matter.
And instead of stabilizing, like a
shadow stuck to its cause, these forms grew jewels,
activated to absorb and reflect.

36   "These jewels flashed in defiance of the real;
matter's endless pit was now encrusted.
I perceived all this, though I could not see.
I did not know that then. I went straight home
and I began to paint a new series.

37   "Speaking to you now, I look back on the
years that followed as the most important
of my life. Inside of them, I despaired.
I was like a spirit formed by a witch,
performing tasks whose ends were unknown.

38   "Even if I were able to know them,
were they the fulfillment of my airy
bondage? Until this moment, the deepest
I had seen into the world was its skin,
a slight vibration forever melting.

39   "I was progressing but my paintings stunk.
The dandruff collecting on my black shirts
said more about an object's relation
to itself and the world than my own work.
I stopped going out. I stopped seeing friends.

40 "Rather than give up, I believed my quest
to be the holiest. Something out of
Balzac—I would die in a fire and all
of my paintings burned except one. My last.
I loved being young; I do not miss it.

41 "I was headstrong. I didn't know that my
invention was imitation. I had
worked to dissolve the borders of the world
only to infect myself with gestures
meant to elide, convince, and implicate."

42 "Let's have dessert outside." Clarice collects
dirty plates. Noa opens the front doors
and leads the group out. Katherine, happy,
stays and conscripts awestruck Kevin to wash
dishes. We sit comfortably at dusk.

43 The open upstairs window lets smudged child
voices into the dark yard that mix with
leaves moved by the wind our less subtle skin
cannot feel to lay a mid-range bed for
Kat's high laughter and Deray's low chest voice.

44 That night I heard their two stories at once,
in stereo. At first, I recognized
how differently they performed ego
and believed this difference to stem from
their character. Now I know I was wrong.

45   They spoke in parallel but I will break
them apart. We've heard Deray speak our first act
and now Katherine enacts the second,
enlivened by Kevin's youthful questions.
Assume their hands are busy: soap, sponge, rag.

46   She allows Kevin to begin. Softly,
"How long have you known . . ." "Noa and Clarice?
Oh god, forever. Since college at least."
"UofC?" "No." She leaves him her silence.
Control established, a flirtation starts.

47   "Just your basic dull Midwestern college,
liberal arts majors from the mid-sized
cities their nice parents ended up in."
More silence.
                She waited, smiling, for him.
He knew what to do with young insouciance . . .

48   . . . but this? A bubble of bitter lemon
soap pops near his open mouth to coat
his tongue in hazy chemicals, ". . . like when I
would follow my sisters into the bathroom
and choke on cheap endless hairspray," he said.

49   "I never used it when I was younger,
except," she said, "when I was in a play."
"My sisters must have tried every product
on me. I was that goofy boy who had
frosted tips in third grade. My mom was so . . .

50 embarrassed. She was a hippie, couldn't
understand her chic daughters," Kevin said.
He looked up from the plate he was drying.
"It was weird. Going between them," he said.
"Did you settle arguments, or?" she said.

51 "They weren't arguments, just different
types of exegesis," he laughed. "Honest
discussion of initial principles
of understanding, but reborn each night
as a series of unknowable acts."

52 Kat's insides warmed. He spoke like a student.
"Daily life was a constant revelation;
Sarah bought new purple makeup or
Elise had done a lazy job mopping.
My mother saw willed accident as hate."

53 "I remember my teen years peering through
my bedsheets," Katherine said, "trying to
taste the level of dread in the still house
so when I left my room I could be able
to absorb or diffuse. I always failed."

54 "Did you have siblings?" he said. "No, just me,
figuring out my persona through friends
at school and the low-key suggestions mom
deployed when she wasn't meditating.
Even in dread, we always got along."

55   "Is she still alive?" he said. "Still with us.
We see each other through the baby now.
When I was younger, she'd take me to lunch
or coffee and we'd each slowly devolve,
taking turns telling stories until we

56   met in our family's emotional
limbo, the astral plain built with symbols
only we know, only we care to know,
so that we could climb the ego ladder
to see how the cycles repeat," she said.

57   "It took hours. So we'd switch from coffee
to tea then tea to wine or beer or a
martini. With her I could unbecome
myself. I can't say what it was for her.
The hidden mother. I'm sure I'll know soon.

58   "Do you like heist movies? I suppose all
boys do . . ." (with this naming he blushed, as he
was meant to do) . . . "I always felt I was
in one when I was twenty, a young girl
made up of a team of useless experts.

59   "I'd become one of them for a month, then
another, a series of personas
with indeterminate goals as real as
the world, but only to them. An escape
artist with a parent on life support,

60   "the bombmaker saving for retirement,
or, my favorite, the young safecracker
silently producing terms of revenge.
I'd spend months passive to some unsold script,
fulfilling nothing but a hack's dreams,

61   "waiting, not knowing I was waiting, for
a phone call from a shadowy contact
to become an operative in a
larger conflict between agencies I
wouldn't know about until the last act.

62   "This was all inward, but it affected
my speech, or my speech's intent. These people . . ."
Kat paused to drink wine. Kevin kept silent.
"My mother hid, or seemed to hide, the words
that would lead to an effortless end.

63   "The guilt I felt, my thought destroyed speech then.
My house, my roommates, old friends, a party.
Secrets passing between doors, new lovers
drunk in a corner. Fashion of the young.
The way forward, drunken levitation.

64   "But the remembered detail, next morning,
in line at the diner. Colin bragging
about how he tossed a red cup across
the room into the trash and saw beneath
its end-over-end arc a lazy grope.

65 "I stood within this act's memorial.
    Then, as now, I cannot see the couple's
    faces that inlaid those objects—hand, ass—
    with such arrogant, mean purpose. I could
    just see their negligence and feel its cost."

66 Kevin was now drying with great fervor.
    "Without their faces, what am I trying
    to describe to you now, what I saw then,
    It's not empathic projection, I'm sure.
    This image . . . this symbol from an image . . .

67 ". . . their negligence was born out of bodies
    that were already in the world even
    without my perception of them, even
    without total knowledge of their movement,
    or total knowledge of their dark intent.

68 "Suddenly our table number was called.
    I had never liked to eat sweet breakfast
    but that day I gorged on pancakes piled high
    with sweet cream and jam, honey and syrup.
    I drank a sickly vanilla latte.

69 "As my friends and new friends gossiped and ate,
    the sweets congealed into a lengthy speech
    on the origin of love within the
    joint culpability of two objects.
    A springing forth rather than a coming to.

70   "I've thought about what I would have said then
     many, many times over the years. I've
     written book after book grasping after
     my hungover starch-and-maple-infused
     monologue and, while I have gotten close,

71   "I've never been able to draw the full
     circumference. This was silent knowledge
     that I overheard; I was the farmer
     in an old tale trusted with the baby,
     the secret king I would raise to be true.

72   "I do know this. It was an argument
     in a series that was not a series.
     Simultaneous flashes in order.
     Spatial agreement meant to be performed
     with belief as end instead of knowledge,

73   "like something from Dante's purgatory,
     though I had neither sinned nor suffered nor
     walked the path of those that had to witness,
     next to my master, the sculptures given
     by the true right hand, revealed by lightning.

74   "In my first book I described it like I
     had come upon a well bubbling with
     clear water—to my friends it was nothing
     but the ravings of a jealous young girl
     lost in the reception of the world's gifts.

75   "But what I could not say was that it was
the final break of my bleak attachment
to the symbol of youthful inquiry.
I could no longer join self to early
flesh. At last my body was whole and raw."

76   The dishes are done. Kevin finishes
drying the last pot while Katherine sprays
the remnants of dinner into the drain.
The balancing of the evening's dishes,
the flip of the garbage disposal switch.

77   There is a hesitant moment of eye
contact that, because I could not see them,
I missed at the time, but seems important
to note for *my* story, which you are in.
Deray begins his second act, our third act.

78   "I believe there is no sequence of thought
that cannot be known as rare emotion
dismissed from the earth. Yes, yes, listen to
the artist. You've followed my life story.
Now hear what I've found underneath that life.

79   "I say it again. I believe there is
no sequence of thought that cannot be known
as a rare emotion dismissed from the earth.
Any muddle I found or find myself in
is poor reasoning I add to the earth,

80 "an emotion so specific in its
    intensity that I must see it through
    my body or, in extreme cases of thought
    —those moments of lived experience that
    exist in memory like dreams of fire—

81 "I must see earth through another body."
    Upstairs the children play the Beach Boys. Loud.
    Its interruption allows us to shift
    our small circle inward. It is dark now.
    We cannot see each other. I touch glass.

82 "My new painting took me outside," he said,
    "and instead of looking within to blur
    the edges of the world's objects I stood
    waiting for the objects' own inward glance
    to surprise me with silver radiance.

83 "While I painted I would sing to myself:
        The mist holds the mountains
        The mountains hold The Golden King
        Mist makes the mountains float
        The mountains hold The Golden King

84 "My sight improved but my painting was poor.
    I could not connect world to mind to hand.
    Each—world/mind/hand—portrayed a point-of-view
    lost to each as when improvisors lose
    the dialogue of song and become sound.

85 "In music, out of this wild neglect comes
a new song, even if the discursive
gesture only exists through that lying
witness, the grey mind of the listener.
In my work, this neglect gave me nothing,

86 "not even the lonely silence the heart
gives to our misapprehension of space,
of what's contained in space, and measurement.
I was lucky. I still showed and sold work,
but I grew less content as life settled.

87 "I tried to fix them in installation,
figuring the paintings just needed context.
So many dumb ideas. I'll give one.
A painting of a mountain presented
in front of a picture of a mountain.

88 "I made the same mistake all artists make
in their practice when they should stop and live.
I was a poet reading with samplers
or a photographer taking ballet.
The safe ignorance of the dilletante.

89 "What this type of making must have felt like
when it was still new. I could have become,
like many of my friends, a believer
in constant, cool reassurance from that
vampire, the historical avant-garde.

90 "I was a different type of believer,
one who wanted to know about the world,
all of our human response to it.
To take ballet, learn techno, leave it there.
To find in form something within itself.

91 "So I began looking at painting.
Again. Things I hadn't looked at since I
had braces. Paintings no one would look at.
Paintings no one had seen, that meant little,
or only meant something to teenagers.

92 "When I was younger, first out of grad school,
I was lucky to be asked to dinner
by one of those men who surround all scenes
and, in exchange for anonymity
and good conversation, fund those in need.

93 "I had no sense of how to hold myself.
Which I'm sure he knew. Let's call him Devin.
It was the last month for the restaurant.
The chef, known for quoting philosophers
on his menus, had decided to quit.

94 "He had made his name twenty years prior,
when American restaurant culture
was, somehow, incorporating Europe
while refusing it, like the continent
was the Big Daddy in a Williams play.

95   "Devin knew him, had been his sommelier
early on, and so what was already
opulent was made awesome. And I mean
awesome in the old sense, like when one looks
beneath and sees the grand complication.

96   "But I could not see until the meal's end.
With Devin's conversation food appeared
dissociative. Each fresh bite burst
with new sensation for ten long courses.
Moment to moment, my palate reset.

97   "And then the wine. Wine, to me, was covered
in plastic wrap at the end of the night.
I did not realize it was food too;
it whispered with the belly's bloated words
as much as those shouted by the liver.

98   "Each second, a heavenly counterpoint
I received was overwhelmed by freedom
offered through Devin's new, moneyed friendship.
At the end of the meal the chef brought out
three jellies. Drunk, I savored each alone.

99   "These were the bass notes for that endless meal,
the flavors that gave meaning to it all.
Coming upon Elaine in the darkened
corner of the museum, I knew that
I would never be a painter again."

2

1   "And, I don't know, I guess my question is,
in your conception of things in the world,
is there a difference between object,
symbol, and image?"

                             The grad student paused.
I looked and Lily gave me the high sign.

2   We'd planned ahead. Stuffed our papers in bags
so we could noiselessly exit the hall.
"What a fucking drag . . ."
Lily flew down the steps. "Those cynical . . .
. . . monsters. Careers made from catastrophe."

3   The rental was close, in the teacher's lot.
I watched her change and finished my coffee.
She drove; I opened the dried apricots
and gave them to her, interspersed with nuts.
She mocked philosophy.

4   "These men and their categories . . . so what?!
I'm supposed to rejigger my life's work
to fit some lexical discoveries?
. . . Lily! New words! Tut tut!
And the way they asked questions! Such jerks."

5   I gave her some cherries
and watched the mossy world around us climb.

Our love is built on a series of crimes.
I put on *Bachelor No 2*.
The road ended at the old dairy.

6   We had left early enough that the dew
held and marked my suede shoes. *Not meant for hiking.*
Anyways, I owned nothing for hiking.
We passed through the ruins of the old farm.
Again the green earth rose

7   and we followed it up
until the Pacific appeared below.
I watched a hawk float, hunting, then a pup
appeared along the trail
and led us forward, where we were to go.

8   The dog's owner: a man named Abigail.
We had just begun, but he offered
water and we took it.
"Excuse me if it seems comical,
but can I talk to you two while we sit?"

9   Lily and I, usually inured
from gafflers like this, sat down and listened.
I watched another bird
come up from below and lost it in the sun.
"Except to Labneh here, I barely speak."

10   I confess, except for this first sentence
and the section I'm about to tell you
(which, for beauty, I've tweaked)

I cannot remember his impromptu
monologue. I'll say this. It was unique.

11 He went on and on with no repentance.
I waited for Lily to start to squirm
for the second time that day, but unlike
her response to the men of the conference
she let the moment churn.

12 Watching her, I heard the bald men yell "Strike!"
in the next lane the first time we hung out.
Two teams of mixed acquaintance getting drunk.
Lucien, Sarah, this little fucker Mike.
Steven and Jane and then Christine the punk.

13 I'd met her through Rebecca at the park.
Sean handed us polishes and sauerkraut,
took Rebecca away. We talked till dark.
Then . . . we forget. Lost at the bar no doubt.
Suddenly, renting shoes

14 with a group of my secondary friends
(for whatever reason, I love bowling,
and so choose it over better events
in my calendar) watching men toweling
balls and howling, acting like tough guys, then

15 Lily, sitting with the more gorgeous Sam,
who all night I wished would leave so I
would only have Lily to occupy
my thoughts and my eyes and my speech. Steven,
the other single dude, was in heaven

16   and, being much louder, quickly chose sides.
It has taken me years to understand
how the rational system diagrams
the world when we are young. The thought young pride
gives to thought's known map—

17   the whispers charted areas give life
that propose all inborn motion lies
in tradition—misses the overlap
thought causes when space takes time as a wife.
But age slowly unwraps

18   the discoveries, postulates, and lies
each generation stifles the next with
till the overlap yields
and true dark motion bubbles up to steal
young thought as new demons learn to theorize.

19   True abstraction is terrifying, not
meant for gallery walls but grown from myth
seeded by the conversation of friends.
Arthur and Lancelot
in shared pursuit of the fire's monolith.

20   There's a Pound poem about two singers—
It is a call from one to another.
"To what lovers will your poetry tend?"
they ask. "My poems will have few lovers.
Most will misapprehend.

21 But weirdos will linger
    over a bookstall's broken paperback
    mouthing words above a dirty finger
    wondering why no one cares for me."
    Those glazed kids who purr the zodiac

22 and live in golden ambiguity
    have always appeared as Lily appeared then:
    lithe, cold, smooth, and in black unwashed clothing.
    I smelled flesh's vacancy;
    without the self, there is no self-loathing.

23 We flirted. The alley's bright halogens
    went dark and ABBA blared.
    Neon lasers and the dank smell of fog.
    In meditation, I've become aware
    my mind led me to this. Never again.

24 She adored prog and she hated Herzog.
    We disagreed on our choice of swill beer.
    Professionally, we were opposites.
    She spoke from her book, *Earth's Green Monologue*,
    I was in moccasins

25 for bands as a vibe tech or engineer.
    Each fact a joke to make the other laugh.
    We moved closer, then over my shoulder
    the young actor appeared.
    "Should we do it? Ask for his autograph?"

26   "It's true, they always look so much older."
Lily's cold hand took mine. She was bolder.
We went to the bar, sent over a shot.
"Hold on, give him this napkin." She wrote fast.
We went back to our lane. "What did you ask?"

27   The actor had lately taken key roles
to shift his image from a boy-next-door
to someone bohemian and self-taught.
A recent turn as Hamlet had fulfilled this goal.
He had learned to enact dim abstract thought.

28   He looked at Lily, bull to matador,
as he drank. The napkin stuck to the glass.
He finished, held his hands wide, mouthed "Thank you."
He read the napkin. His interior
sprung from skin that seemed like a looking glass.

29   Years passed. Writing for a little review
I got to ask him what she had written.
She never told me, never would tell me.
"She never said, what was on the napkin?"
"She wanted secrets only you two knew."

30   Over the steak au poivre he ate daily
with snails in the tourist café in Bourges—
above which I lay alone, dreamlessly,
reliving Lily's death as dramaturge
for some manic art play from 80s downtown,

31   having taken rooms I couldn't afford
to complete my stringer's puff assignment
and see my friend, whose late technique astounds—
the actor evoked Lily, my poor dead
wife: her voice, her gestures, her body's sounds

32   and in so doing became her napkin.
"Why is Hamlet buried a soldier?"
he said. The question was, always would be
the same. Like her, it had already been written.
"My answer was weak-spirited."

33   "I was within my own mythology,
misunderstanding strength played out as fate.
I said, 'Sometimes history gets things wrong.'
She just laughed. Lily was so obstinate,
our friendship built out of her scrutiny."

34   "Who Says a Funk Band Can't Play Rock?!" came on.
He put a butter-boiled snail on his fork.
"That night," he said, "we got pissed on your lawn,
bringing out the couches like college dorks.
At your house that night, she didn't tell?"

                                              "No."

35   Have you ever been to a house party
with a famous person? They never go
but somehow, finally, they disappear.
Alone, Lily and I drank mushroom tea,
fucked, then fed each other pistachios.

36 Over breakfast planned the rest of our lives.
    Went to the movies, snuck in our own beer.
    Ate tacos near her house. Cream puffs arrived.
    "My answer now," he said, "is more sincere,
    and must come through a dialogue with you."

37 He became Lily. The café withdrew,
    turned into the alley, then my bedroom.
    He played himself and her; I, myself.
    Her eyes. I heard her in our old bedroom.
    Her voice, in whispers, suddenly, I knew.

38 *Fort.*   Let four captains   400
    Bear Hamlet like a soldier to the stage,
    For he was likely, had he been put on,
    To have prov'd most royal; and for his passage,
    The soldier's music and the rite of war
    Speak loudly for him.   405

39 "Why did he bury Hamlet a soldier?"
    Lily's voice came to me through a strange flesh
    in stopped time. Whatever had been his self
    was a resonant version of her self
    that my mind held and his body possessed.

40 This was the thing that I had to tell her:
    *That the earth was dying, that we needed
    to have a child*. But she interrupted.
    "There will be no war. He has succeeded.
    He sees Hamlet as his own amateur."

41   Discussion when the mind is disrupted
      by the world's miracles will always be
      unfortunate and sad. Only my speech
      would keep her alive. "You think he demeans
      Hamlet?" I said. "That's frivolous. Corrupt."

42   "Yes, but it allows an actor to reach
      for death as if it was the final lie."
      There she was, drinking, giving me the eye
      while making fun of me. Each to each,
      herself: "Can we speak about Fortinbras
      without speaking of Hamlet's portrayal?"
      Actor in thrall of academia.
      "Screw portrayals. Are *they* antipodal?
      Are the two men separate phenomena
      or does the play force them (us) to compete?"

43   Then I saw the conversation's deceit,
      the honeysuckle placed in the pine tree
      by the wind: his eyes flickering between
      his, hers. The beginning of my concrete
      belief in second-level sorcery.

44   To me, Tennyson in aquamarine:
          With a half-glance upon the sky
          At night he said, "The wanderings
          of this most intricate Universe
          teach me the nothingness of things."

45   As I read this upon my mind, my queen
     and the actor became a new body,
     a child, my child, our child, full youth serene,
     to flaming youth let virtue be as wax
     I in them became nothing, nobody.

46   My lack layered in hers like sardonyx
     from the soul's palace. Life, sudden, complete.
     Then they began to talk to me, *father*,
     in the eerie flat voice of politics.
     Competitive and laced with fat deceit.

47   "To speak of them as inverted brothers
     forces us to admit Shax's removal
     of parental unity. So, rather
     than locating Hamlet, in some other
     family," my child said, "what we gather

48   will be, we sense, in search of approval
     of a psyche confused by its models.
     I don't mean to repeat that irony
     runs the play, but that the myth is modal:
     Orestes reads American novels."

49   Like others their age, they spoke sullenly.
     What could I do to help? Become the scrawny
     bedroom musician of my ancient youth
     and speak from behind my mod album sleeves?
     If I could not be seen, I could play Truth.

50   "But how has Time structured how *you* believe?"
Their response astonished their jaded Dad.
I mistrusted the actor's palimpsest.
My child lost sad speech; they weren't naïve.
In my heart they began to manifest.

51   "Consider when theatricality
is compared to its twin sincerity.
Shax reading Montaigne on our changing moods
knew that consistency requires acting."
I interrupted. "I'm not finished, dude . . ."

52   They smiled and I smiled. "Current thought distracts.
Keep the real Globe Theatre in your mind.
The tense plots of Revenge Plays are exact.
They make us wait for hours after rich meals
for death and the actors to intertwine.

53   When a theatrical boy—Hamlet— steals
such a play, effects seem undeserved,
cheap because not justified by the plot.
But theatrical behavior unseals
the self, gives being away for pleasure.

54   So Hamlet must be what the play is not.
He is 'the capacity to astonish.'
He is a hinge: the life-like performer
who is doubly inconsistent, demure
and greedy. Theatrical and distraught."

55 My inclination was to admonish,—
having learned from Lily critical jest.
But I saw new love reading Percy Bysshe
Shelley, alone and overwhelmed by verse,
bundling heart in mind in muscle in chest.

56 And I saw I'd have no time to rehearse
the father archetype I'd been asked to take
to touch—really touch—their chest and release
a noxious monument to my mistakes.
My hunchbacked scholar's body is perverse!

57 Hold them in as nothing but still dim mind
and turn their skeleton into metal.
Muscle and blood mix to make verdigris.
Love's gesture releases them from their bind.
Without thought, touch their chest with grace and ease.

And I looked at Lily.
And Lily looked at me.
And Abigail spoke.

58 "I drove a black motorcycle
across the country to the Bay.
It was Sixty-Eight. Easter Day.
I came out. Gabriel and Michael.

59 In those days you were shown secret
brilliant green doors on warehouse streets
where bull men made in mold from Crete
formed duets, trios, or sextets.

60   Gabriel and Michael and me
       played the stacked jukebox, smoked cigars
       and made our group more modular
with honking drunks. Depravity.

61   In the gold grey dawn I wake them
       without end, mind invisible,
       skin takes a collective nibble,
and the flower reveals the stem.

62   Mid-Century American
       rank coffee witness West Coast roasts:
       mugs on chests in bed, eggs and toast.
A walk through the park. Thick lichen.

63   What else could I do but garden?
       What else but learn to feed love well?
       See their knees in jeans parallel.
Table set as parfait hardened.

64   There is nothing but discussion,
       gossip at the end of the world.
       I add to their soup bowls a swirl
of cream. They're content. I'm blushing.

65   Do you know Nauman's *Studies for
       Holograms*? I have seen them hung
       in an azure hallway, among
thumb-sized sketches of troubadours.

66 I followed their bald collector
  to find them in mind's middle ground
  bordering both hands as he bound
me and thought's rough, raw-wool texture.

67 Nauman's flashed manipulations
  of the face by unknown fingers
  flanked by miniature singers
fixed body/thought's undulations.

68 I still prize these pictures that arc
  through me in juxtaposition
  during sex's blank repetition.
But what then purged all else is now dark.

69 What do I mean? That first his face,
  then those songs sung by costumed men
  dimmed; body/thought's equestrian
shape had long quit. I was unlaced,

70 suddenly alone in moonbeam.
  I was loved in the seventies,
  watched my friends die in the eighties
and received life from both these streams.

71 What is recollection without
  regret? I have none, lack nothing
  lying in memory's soothing
bath. It draws from my present's spout.

72 I don't want my has-been ideal.
      It came to me, I gave to it,
      blessed change came, and here I sit,
alone, at the edge, in the real.

73 I am not free of my past, nor
      does it interlace with the birds
      hunting mice from the air. My words,
I speak, think, and also the tor.

74 Not a has-been ideal but a
      has-been real, the sighting of which
      I give to this world bewitched
by sun instead of Milky Way.

75 Both real, but only the many
      can be seen at once with the eye
      and so the one becomes a shy,
unseen note without harmony.

76 I found this scrap in my reading
      and defined myself against it
      by beginning with it to spite
Keats' lyric essay succeeding:

77 Keats to Bailey, March 13th, 1818
      I am sometimes so very sceptical as
      to think Poetry itself a mere Jack
      a lanthern to amuse whoever may
      chance to be struck with its brilliance.

As Tradesmen say everything is worth
what it will fetch, so probably every
mental pursuit takes its reality and
worth from the ardour of the
pursuer—being in itself a nothing.

78 I allow I am a nothing,
    refuse mind to pursue nothing,
    feel ardour and worth for nothing,
nothing may take from me nothing.

79 My Gabriel and my Michael
    gasping in hospice now appear
    in the burnt glaze of atmosphere
beyond ours in epicycle.

80 Beheld in star times' parousia
    being's worth blinding without me
    to witness yet I also see
their presences' lollapalooza.

81 And so pictures dim but become,
    grasped as one does an animal,
    some other object beyond all,
whose struck silver eye-contact numbs.

82 Life's strange concordance with strange life
    not smudged by dark space but made bright
    in relation to satellites
now brothers, husbands, sisters, wives.

83   What do these star signs give me?
       That Pythagorean number
       gives pleasure like a cucumber
   salted by all airy bodies.

84   Green locus of light and matter,
       a figure of numbered points placed
       by the logic of her cold grace
   fired by inner oscillator.

85   Behind this real then her more real
       of whom all songs you hear are sung
       to make you old, to make you young.
   I'll let you go, here is her seal."

86   Abigail sat straight and began to sing,
   their voice plainer than my coarse retelling.
   I'll end this section with its gift to you,
   one among these blank stars I'm gathering
   that poor reason reduces to three blues.

87   "How long is this
   posthumous life
   of mine to last?

88   Well then one part
   of me must be
   distance,
   routine activities.

89 And another part must be
light
or heat
and a system
for containment.

90 Now,
through eras of presence
I lay myself beside myself.

91 The hand
that points
I dip in silver
filigree I get
by economic
chemistry,

92 blessed memories matter makes up.

93 From Old Hammer-hand's Cookbook
Melody Confronted by Titan
Step 1) Churn nous
Step 2) Bake by fire
Step 3) Careful, the slicer
Step 4) Eat infinity forever

94 So then the twin,
the drunk parent,
the drunk lover,
the fountain filled with gold.

Bred against contempt
elitism, satanism
everything that's rotten
about rock and roll.

95 No more song.
More people singing,
assembled,
lit by spot built
in time by one hand
hired by panel made
in recursive trial.

96 The human body's built trumpet
natural swing done everyday
through oil slick carpentry
most ass-thetes call the world-
of-things makes best mindmeat
to unsink listening.

97 And I have seen the end
in paint hid behind soft
closing doors of which the cost
kills.

98 This is my perception and it
can be yours too,
after pale struggle with
inward god brought
into throat by medicine named

99 Elaine

say it again

Elaine

I can't hear you

Elaine

one more time

Elaine

fifth point the sigil

Elaine."

1   Young century embalms
    fascination. Katherine,
    Kat, extends herself
    above hearth.
    Girls in bed recede.
    Geoffrey, babe, & baseball recede.
    Subway stop for another child, an
    evening with meaning.

2   There is a green stairway
    and there is a light
    and "There Is a Light
    That Never Goes Out" is playing
    loudly to mark
    to interlopers who may
    want
    to achieve friendship
    for the night
    or forever
    or whatever.

3   Black chairs,
    some filled,
    surround Kevin with programs in loft's center.
    His raised brow over tortoiseshell.
    Their chatter briefly quickens
    her heart.
    But the play first, love game later.

4   Program in her hand, drawing
     of a stage: a large circle
     w/ double circumference. Btwn
     2 arcs is written:

      This is the watyr
      a bowte the place

Crude castle drawn w/in inner circle.
Above:

      The castel of perserveranse.
      Let no man sytte ther
      for lettynge of syt,
      for ther schal
      be the best of all.

Small bed beneath castle w/ legend:

      Mankynde is bed
      & ther schal
      the sowle lye
      under the bed
      tyl he schal
      ryse & playe.

5   Performance titled:

THE AMERICAN MUSICAL

6   It'd been two weeks since the gathering.
Deray's appearance under
ersatz stage lights
brings to Kat's mind
the sudden thickness of certain television actors
who'd spent
summer months for the first time
with money to prepare their bodies
for the Season Two opener hoping
to dismiss slender memories or goose
powerful watchers
to hire them,
as if flesh's area is
to attention conjured
equal to a larger screen.

7   Later   Deray said, "I've wanted,"
to Kat as Kat watched Kevin
play pool w/ his friends at
the dive bar down
the road,
"to think the musical
for so long.
Make it part of my
performative body so that my mind might
be let loose of it as myth and let it live
instead as life.

8   "I do not mean myth.
I have

no quarrel

with myth.

I mean the reception

of knowledge that might otherwise be called

folk history,

by which I mean the *facts* of how

we tell each other how we got here—

the aggregation of story Tolstoy,

borrowing terms from Newton,

found in the refusal of Napoleon made clear through

the image

of an overweight intellectual named Pierre

walking

the streets of Moscow with a knife, rather than

the slash of light that unfolds the bath

of the real

nursing

individual.

9   "I have never been interested in the ensemble,

or, I am interested in

the ensemble when

it presents itself in the figure of

an actor. "One."

A Chorus Line's signature song as a presentation of,

as a forced projection of,

the director,

Zach.

I've always seen the one not

built up

of different voices but one
collapsing
into
many
different voices."

10   Kat laughed,
slugged her shot,
thought of Leibniz,
smiled at Kevin,
knocked back the end of the Old Style,
held fingers up, glanced,
asking, at Deray,
who nodded,
ordered them another round,
and paid for the shots and beers
from the stack of bills dwindling
on the bar.
"Running Up That Hill" began on the jukebox.

11   "I began by imagining the ending
of an act, an ensemble singing to confront
their choices to change and leave
an audience mulling
over intermission.
I brought this emotional pitch as a series of voices
into which an actor could fall
to present
a beginning
of historical life

for emotion extended
in time.
To not upend
or reinvent but to live
with the determination of victims ignored and otherwise subsumed,
those immigrants and Blacks always
downstage—
in the musical gesture but never
more than ghosts made present
in song.

12 "In lonely rehearsal this ensemble number became
an out-of-the-blue-number; moments
of shared inward clenching
worked through in tandem
across the stage suddenly
           called
up the early gasps of future fresh built
on the refusal of
the present   represented   in air   by song   itself.
My voice
now polyvalent,
now diachronous,
found its only diagetic escape:
a conditional past coming to be through consequence,
as the century's slow
righteous blossom brought
to matter   some new memory of
a short walk up
a tall hill to see

the foreign country's famous monastery now
empty   and unused   except
for the tombs
for which you count
unfamiliar coins   to light
by electric candle.

13   "My character had not stepped aside.
They had not gone under themselves to find
gestural competence from
interlocking parts within nor   did they float
to some   ideal height
of continuous presentiment
     but found
simultaneously mapped
onto the space of its body more bodies
not to be worked through or smeared
into some continuity borrowed
from those novels and plays that love theory
more than life we read
as aging children looking
for new parents but that
staccato voice we   can only   call

THE SOUL

   now made
strange by not being theirs,
                or, rather, mine,
settled as it was   on many thrones rubbed

smoothed by sand
more colorful than   that naughty thing   of dew, air, and light
—the rainbow—
          might dream to present to the eyes of those
struck dumb by the influence
                    of the facts
of an overweight caterpillar.

14   "In rehearsal   a voice spoke
through me   in the sensual   phrasing of
prime country
          music crossed
with the insistent syntax   of early blues   over
the rhythm of imported European patter.
By arguing   backwards I sang   the origin
of   contemporary American   song and knew, as
those Italian men did, who argued   behind walls no wifi
would ever pierce over   the interpretation of
Greek texts, that   the bondage
of music to word captured the ritual of
                    wisdom   (as such)
in transference   of content through form undoing
ages of   form presented as appearance from beyond
          to make
     the unrecognizable human tongue manifest
                         &
               that
                              the discovery of opera
          that
                              the discovery of the musical

that

the discovery of interdisciplinary performance

was retrieval,

not birth."

15   Kat quotes the *Popol Vuh*:

"Here their father is put back
together by them. He wanted his
face to become just as it was,
but when he was asked to name
everything, and once he had found
the name of the mouth, the nose,
the eyes of his face, there was
very little else to be said.
Although his mouth could not
name the names of each of his
foreign parts, he had at least
spoken again."

16   "Exactly," Deray said, laughing.
"Dreams of history are built on precognition.
What books beside the Mayan must be read
to fill time w/ names? Pound,
periplum aboard   his ship can present
eras as if   happening "out there" but
they still figure the map   of his mind.
    What else lays under the map of the world, ignored
                    &
        what manifests dirt of actual earth

&
what speaks when soul calls
&
why must they always sing?"

17   Kevin catches up
as Katherine leaves the bar.
They walk the two blocks
        that split
        the bar w/ his flat
                and flirt.

He offers.

But she believes in the
distance
        of dreams

and lets him go
        with a "no"
    confused with a peck and a
small, accidental—he will never know,
or see her again—
        tap below
            the belt.

18   Katherine's mind now.
Her walk
home.
I disappear.
So should you.

19   Bar time. Chicago
      street, television: synonymous.
      Weekly human errors
      in bright contagious
      light.

20   Tend north, northwest, darkness I eliminate.
      Out only different light, of one
      intellect, matter made by
      imagination holding
      world in sight.

21   That boy,   attractive
      young Kierkegaard,
      fits past's gaps.
      My overlaid '90s desire
      for another young boy.
      William, in bed, reading
      badly spoken German:

> Du bist vollbracht
> Nachtwache meines Daseins.

The stuttered translation:

> You are fulfilled,
> nightwatch of my life.

Mad scruffy pretension reaching
always out of ignorance.

22 Wild how self
    re-presents self.
        Mind is strata so intellect breeds
    out of   compressed time. My light now
    Leibniz layered onto Søren, in love.
    Who I am + Who I was
            —twins otherwise—
    find a third in their fusion.

        Outside.

    There she is, made by *mes*, cannot
    touch her but I can sing, harmonize.
    Separate
    literal me in
    that third's melody.

23 Late night grad school with William. His voice:

            Transeunt actions of created things their
            agreement divine
            preformation accommodating each
            thing to things
            outside of itself and
            to the union of
            soul and body.

    The mistakes of my lovers and me.
    Future, present, past, imagined discussion.
    In them actual thought comes to be:

not poetry à philosophy
not philosophy à poetry
but
each intertwined in space
in me
&
out of me
as those characters

in me and out of me
&
the love made with
(& for)
the world.

24 No time for those who worship symbols
No time for those who worship signs
No time for those who worship abstraction
No time for those who worship mind
No time for those who worship things
No time for those who worship bodies
No time for those who worship performance
No time for those who worship systems
No time for those who worship I
No time for those who worship one
No time for those who worship many
No time for those who worship language
No time for those who worship song

only space
that multitude contained therein of dis-

continuous song
coming to be known in
closed narrative opened
by those closed others.

Narrative space / ever-loving time.

25 William, my love, when
did we last walk
at this hour drunk
in argument over
some minor thing?
A footnote in Locke?
Aside in Hume?
The rhythms of thought in late afternoon,
stoned,
    reading with music.

Windows open.
Shared youth concerned with nothing but itself and
the finding of life
in some kind
of easy labor
meant for kings and queens,
or, at least,
their sons and daughters.

26 William how
you would have loved
Kevin who speaks

with your voice but
to me, old as his mother, asking
to be taken
home and loved like
    he was you
        &
    I was me
        but younger.

William his
mistakes are yours.
I love them still,
I take them home.
        Hide from myself I cannot.
        Turkey cocks ruffle feather at red.
        So it goes with me when I see green.

27   Some have believed   that the sun   is God
but they
did not know that
the fixed stars are suns as well.
Put space   in a basement
      &
    reflect.

There was a house in Ukranian Village.
A bowling alley in Avondale.
Tennis courts in Pilsen or
an abandoned convenience store in the West.
All for us.   All for shows, music & performance.

A system of paper
spread hand to hand,
but mostly whispers
and phone calls to tell   of what's to come.

William seen for days
drinking beer
in a band
of boys. *Not* musicians—
unwashed
culture revelators.

28 How I enjoyed love
as a spectator to him
and myself. The mood
was wonderful. I let
the world have me
in strings of forgotten
songs and the gaffes
of manic hustle
jealously tends.
The neighborhood—my neighborhood—
—our neighborhood—
then undiscovered.
No nonsense like this,
crisp youth brightly lit,
new Bacchanal babes
in clothes we could never afford.
Space shared and time seen,
love, infinite, still finds new packages.

I'm older, I see difference.
Kevin's loft a last outpost of the old shabby love
& creative vectors
birthed on this diagonal street.

29 Twenty-five years ago,
   barely a dank burrito place.
   Now,
   imported street food perfected
   by 2nd generation kids and their
   bearded white boy backers.
   Clubs every inch w/ televised
   draught lists.
   My own lost city in the move
   across the millennium.
   The hand I had in it,
   those of my friends,
   researching Italian cuts,
   the global movement of the dumpling,
   effluence rhythm,
   and the transfer of power through taste.

30   Not a fallen world but life
          falling from time-marked-space
   into space
             where extended mass alone
    is not sufficient
        but the notion of force,
   primitive forces

which contain not only act

or

the completion of possibility

but also

an original activity.

There he was beside me.

Division, a house, west:

Of William who knows

—metempsychosis—

is not generation

but development.

The first day lovers share clothes,

the resuscitation of drowned flies buried in chalk.

31 How many musics of my body?

. . . my mind?

. . . my soul?

How many crescents of light

guess a more whole shape

made from darkness?

We lie and listen,

William and me,

no a/c.

Form between us, but some other form.
Songspeech
of '90s Chicago summer.

Overture
is prophecy
in relation
to opera.

32 The count,
the counting song,
the list of lovers,
their styles abstracted,
consciousness exposed,
the consistent mien,
heavy sense cradled dead.

        or

The less embattled twin,
w/ stalking,
pathetic release,
aria of madness,
winter's darkness,
the consistent mien,
blithe creation insisted.

33 *Down on the street where the faces shine*,
William, the O-Mind,

the mental state of the unit,
collective mind.
I see a pretty thing, ain't no wall
learned in some Iggy bio,
Emerson in Detroit.

Now in William waking
to seize my sense,
how that room
became a cosmos.

no walls no walls no walls

The door out, into his arms, a mirror
deep in the night I'm lost in love
looking up, past the Chicago common brick,
drunk walks done no scurry behind sense
a thousand lights look at me

34 Aging woman's resistance
to the common trouble of entertainment.
How dumb boys are.
The white belt in and out of style.
Decisions made across fanzines, touring bands.
The losers more attractive. No real fascination
with the common and rather inward-looking.
Always that belief in the shifting surface
of the eternal within, how they suddenly
found themselves thirty,   eternities
tuned to the present,

his gestures as a man of lectures,
and my eyes still seeking discussion,
blind to how I steered other voices.
Dance became pedagogy.

35 Each date endless, the wine dis-embalming
love's habit till dessert brought
safe rhythm sheathed in dreams of death.

Years of inferential argument disproving axioms of time.

I now know the future has nothing to do with the past,
that procession is break,
poetry becomes myth becomes narrative becomes the novel,
and life is a series of lives,
miniature autobiographies told by different characters
inhabited by a reader
reading the text of a speech written
by an author who cannot speak.

36 The false blur of memory contains us,
but generations of dubbing distorts the master,
legs up in boots on the mixing desk
believing ourselves to be free in songs
William'd written to mark revelatory moment
that my added guitar had given life.
The second pass over always more real,
more understood,
though more distant in time
and no more part of us than thought.

37 Turn off Milwaukee, the streets grow dark
    except where houses blot the shrubs of small
    city-gardens with energy-safe fluorescent.
        America slathers
        self-hatred on all of us.
        Guilt in ability or inability,
        what is there or isn't,
        flagellation to be done by all,
        toward and away from life.
        When done,
        what new matter
        to despise.

38 I say out of love's death only better love.
    There, through the window, Geoffrey is
    on our couch, ready to receive
    some part of it, letting the rest go.
    More love for dim creation,
    as if our nothings could be held instead of filled
    with the insouciant screams of inherited murder:
    "If I cannot become myself, neither can you."

39 That symbol,
    the retina,
    the bed where we meet
    to vibrate air
    like the hummingbird.

40 And I make it too,
    the green eternal leaf
    upside-down in the white willow.

And I make it too,
the wreath,
the chain of changeable red.

And I make it too,
a third un-named kef
where the rose used to stand.

I make it too.

41 The wedding was, no, *is* a point in time.
          Geoffrey and me,
          other people's concentrations.
          A ritual to refuse transaction as determinate.
But there we are
representing everyone's transformation.
I stepped out of the book
to release our chains
for a bright weekend
of room-temp platters
signaling chatter.

I can measure the infinite in three children
sleeping while Geoffrey struggles, drunk on half a beer,
with a video game about demons.

42 Life bare,
he finds a save point.
We kiss, sneak onto the deck
with baby monitor, last beers.
"There's still breast milk in the fridge,

she's down for another hour at least."
This is where we talk.
I cannot tell you what we say.
It is mine.
Instead, I will tell you three stories, with a framing narrative,
to end the night,
dessert to end the meal.

Imagine me nursing my child in the early morning sun.

43 Before time or space,
    at the edge of our yet-imagined universe
    there is darkness,
    what we now call darkness,
    but then had no name,
    and I call them Aeschylus.

44 On the edge of the universe, Aeschylus is in the midst.
    Matter and abstraction, imagination and dreams
    of generation
    hold darkness' extension.
    Things live on the other side of the edge,
    where what we are is yet to be.
    A turtle's clothes are a house;
    it lives in the world.

45 Eons of loneliness like frozen night-times
        of stress' threat.
    Then, Aeschylus recognizes a twin across the border
        and each is brought

into themselves by the other
　　as buttons
fumbled by fourteen-year-old lovers.
Aeschylus and Sophocles leap unity
　　to amend nothing
with two.

46　Suddenly stars
　　of different size
are bounced
　　from one twin
to the other.
　　Games exist. Joy.
Now the gestation of the one
　　by subtracting their difference.
The score is five to four,
Euripides, the concrete one of the two,
　　comes to make three.

47　Three means one is never stronger than two.
New twins, politics and story, reign.
Ball games serve no purpose,
fallow stars abound.
"The stars are life we don't need anymore.
　　Let's arrange them for others."
They agree on a new game, the winner
　　is the arranger.

48　Each will tell one story.
They who speak with the most truth,

according to the others,
will arrange the stars.
    I do not know
how darkness draws straws,
    but it is done,
and Sophocles begins.

Remember their only rule as you read:
    Judge what is most true.
Beware the false true story.

49 STORY ONE

Sophocles:

In the shade of glass structures
    made eons ago by an extinct race of mad giants
a group of ants retire after dinner
    for cigars,
        drinks,
            and shaved ice flavored
by a fruit known only to the small.
So far the party has been frivolous,
    but as antennae lose their outer range of
        invisible sense,
the group focuses on an argument between a group of four:
        a red ant,
        a black ant,
        a winged ant,
        and a queen.

        The theme is justice.

With encouragement each ant speaks extemporaneously.

50 No records were kept,
         but when I spoke
to an ant who had been
   in attendance at lunch
the following day—having stayed home myself
         to write genre fiction embezzled
with existential themes into the early
   hours of the morning—
they gleefully described   the speeches to me.
     "The black ant spoke first
     of generations of knights
     keeping order in the land.
     One day, the greatest knight
     rides out of the castle in search
     of the active protection
     of chivalry. Right before
     the field becomes the wood
     is a fountain on which two adepts
     sit arguing. The knight stops
     and asks to help them.

51   "One tells a story involving property.
     The other tells a story involving family.
     They are the same story.
     Due to the great knight's action,
     both of their heads fall into the fountain.
     Plumes of red water frame the blue sky
     to create an illusion of green.
     The great knight continues into the forest.

Then the red ant gave a speech
highlighting a rock who eats, about which
the less said, the better.
The winged ant's speech, however, is worth retelling.

52   'Imagine endless swamp along a coast,'
the winged ant began.
'One moonless night a woman of brown moss comes
to the bed of a single man.
In the morning they eat a quiet breakfast
of salted fish, hard bread, eggs, and espresso.
The man takes the day off and they sit
on the porch of his floating house and watch
the clouds. The moss woman recites
a poem of contentment
grooved in the gauzy shadow of the symbols of her kin.
As she finishes, her body begins to oscillate,
suddenly alive with the bugs and small animals
that call her home. The man embraces her
to prove his love and as they part he holds in his arms
a crying baby, born from his belly.
All that is left of her is a stick bug who doffs
his Tyrolean hat
and blesses the child
in the manner
of the country.

53   'From the day they can hold a rod,
the sexless child is a fisher of genius.
Their family becomes an important one.
Soon the father is king

and his child a groundbreaking teacher,
self-help guru, and writer of the masterpiece of autofiction
in three volumes, *The Quivering Line*.

The king grows old. He is now blind.
He becomes obsessed with creating a sculpture
of the moss woman in dark clay.
The child helps him. The king dies with two
hands gripping the face of his long-disappeared
lover, thumbs in the eyes, fingers curled around the ears.
The next morning, the child-king invents fire,
burns their father and mother,
and overflows the swamp with gold coins
until rivers become city-streets for the accursed.'

54 "Last, the queen.
She performed a toast,
thanked the host.
I was able to write down
her short speech,
which I will read to you now.

'I have built a ladder
where no natural ladder occurs
and in the earliest darkness of the eastern sky
my flesh is mirrored from the street.
My corrupt breath
no longer raises the idle cat.
Take this ladder or kill me,
the choice is easy enough.'"

STORY TWO

Aeschylus:

It is a vile age in hindsight,

where a plurality of the planet's citizens

support the election of a robot

invented for execution

by living blobs of small mind

who have slowly consolidated power

as they've consolidated bodies

—blobs being little attendant

to meat's borders—

in the hopes of converting

skeletons into building materials for cities

centered on the low culture

of the only flesh.

56 Out of power for at least another generation

the skeletal responded as all downtrodden do:

arguing their case through cultural expression

to free the spirits of the bony

while attracting

rebellious globual intellectuals.

Production was unstoppable.

The ascension of a movement took weeks,

it was forgotten in a weekend.

From the beginning there was

a split between New Historicists, who felt

that stiffness could only be spoken

through a recapitulation of blobbish gestures

shot through with critical insertions of stable nuance

or the refashioning of secret bone heroes
hiding in plain sight at the margins
of fleshy culture, and The Osseinists, who believed
the spine was effable only in the refusal
of all past through
the realization of utopia
in aesthetic vision.
Fame made through contrasting idealisms.

57   Somewhere besides the planet's sites of cultural exchange,
a southern capital or a northern metropolis,
lived a group of skeletal artists
who formed a band
named for an obscure, yet common,
bodily function whose repetition here
would lose me the game
on the fair charge of obscenity.
It is important to note
that this band, by all accounts,
totally fucking ruled.

58   While their contribution
has been assimilated into the now-tidy history
of the post-skeletal avant-garde, to witness
this band in their moment
was to come into contact
with the living spine
as it made its way upright
in a universe formed
by that invisible evil,

gravity.
Their performances were known
for dangerous acts that placed
all present into a space of complicity
with life as it *was* rather
than what it *might have been*
or *could be*.

59 As the band, instruments tuned
to what they called
bonal harmony, a scale
of 206 notes made
in relation to the resonant qualities of bone,
played a fierce fusion
of distinct noise
that made a farce
of the world,
their singer, Tex Continuous,
distributed hidden psychedelics into the crowd
with swings of a man-o-war
dipped, in the green room, in laced spinal fluid,
flanked by twins being pierced in reflection
—one first through the skull,
the other through the left baby toe—
until they passed out decorated
in jewelry that recalled
long forgotten ritual still living
in the mind as dream.

60 Without flesh,
the band's summoning of anal energy

was speculative, more like fire

than wood.

The language of the band was the hideous stereotype without irony,

so the naked gristle of the blob's sold and sucked nipple

and the uncontained marrow of the sex bone

linked the body's reservoirs of existential frailty

with all bodies' dark damage, damage pursued in response

to the realization of death as cause rather than effect,

instead of with belief in transcendence through whatever systems

purchased the mind that month, trading,

as well all do,

pennies for yo-yos.

61 Knowing that the martyr was worse than living death,

the authorities left the band alone

until a political director, the blob Stefan,

banished to blob-no-wheres-ville by court frivolities

only he believed in

(in fact, Stefan was a terrible bore),

found his young son and daughter preparing

their toilette in *style contemporain*

by swallowing black market femurs harvested,

no doubt, from the mass graves of the prison camps,

in order to prove to the bouncers at Beerland

that while the toned shapes of their flesh

marked them as offspring of the ruling class,

they were, nonetheless,

friends of the skeleton.

62 This modification had its roots

in their father's, the political director's, generation.

Blobs of that era witnessed daily
public acts of skeletal sadism
and soon sex workers were being tasked
by fraught teenagers
with no models for their proclivities
in popular culture
to make flesh bone.
After a few hours, the skeleton imbibed by the children was excreted painfully.
Most overdoses happened during what was called
'falling out,' when painkillers of any kind
were taken in large quantities
to divorce a blob from the pain of losing bone.
Club kids brought into public
what had been practiced in the backrooms
of high society for years.
Only mothers and fathers were shocked.

63 So Stefan tried power and rounded up Tex.
Stefan sat across from Tex Continuous
in a small grey room made smaller
by a slight window that, rather than
provide light from the world's many suns,
leeched darkness from the cell to spread
into the world.
               Each was willful.
As the interrogation continued into its fifteenth hour,
the enemies leaned closer and closer until, unrestrained
by hatred of each others' systems of being,
their foreheads touched.
The miracles of a new race of flesh and bone

greeted the bored jailor as he entered the next morning
to loud sobbing after their falling out never occurred.
Hatred and cynicism continued in one body
with new objects to describe."

64 **STORY THREE**

Euripides:

The middle forty years of Tomaz's life
had coincided with the country's modernization.
At eighteen there was only the possibility of becoming a man in the field.
Then revolution, counter-revolution, and the promise
of a global revolution saw him
become a soldier, an intellectual, spy,
dissident, exile, public intellectual, newspaper
editor, political director, advisor on public relations,
prisoner, and then, again, a man in the field.
After a long day, he wrote articles for encyclopedias about dead
friends and ideas.
While the country—if not Tomaz's place in it—
had stabilized, at its borders sat a group
of men who too thought they could be distinguished
through violence.

65 In the simple house in the far east was a stove,
a bed, and a long table that Tomaz and his wife,
Vera, sat at all day, writing.
In the cool evenings of the late summer they would walk
after dinner discussing nothing
but their love and the work that went on beside it:
her novels, his articles. There was no money

and they shared bread with their neighbors,
coming together on Fridays to smoke and dance.

66   Like Tomaz, Vera had many careers.
When the broken sons and daughters of their neighbors
began returning from the front
her past as a doctor returned.
Soon, an ersatz hospital was set up
in an abandoned barn. Tomaz would
accompany his wife to her duties,
reading to the young men and women
when they were awake,
writing his articles on his knee while they slept.

67   Vera's novel, now worked on in the mornings and evenings,
began to change. What had begun
as a mannered realist novel retelling
stories from her and Tomaz's past
first became plump and baroque,
then shifted into a farce
starring an undead knight and his squire, a pile of trash,
until finally the book became a fantasy
about a young girl and her talking bear
discovering her true lineage as first
princess, then queen.

68   Then, the winter march.

69   "Blood, not the sun, is where they think life is,"
Tomaz found himself saying at the small gathering

of farmers that served as a weekly market.
Later, with Vera, they agreed
reality was implicitly mythological.
And there were soldiers three towns away,
then two, then one, then over the river
Vera and Tomaz walked along, speaking quietly with their hands.

70   There was nothing to say goodbye to,
everything was coming with them,
but the house held their life
in the first day of fall felt on the bare floor,
pencil shavings missing the trashcan,
and savory pies allowed once a month.
They hid their manuscripts in the carts
with the wounded soldiers, and joined neighbors
walking northeast at the first edge of winter.

71   Retreat and change had become familiar.
Those who could walked, those who couldn't
were helped. Tomaz and Vera lit fires
in the evening and read aloud from whatever
was at hand. Food was scarce but delicious.
A baby was born, one night a marriage,
everyday life was there, in between
long walks to an unimagined home.

72   Those that died were buried, Tomaz
was second to the preacher
in performing rites or speaking
to the remaining family.

Flowers were always found, a small band
played the same piece of music.

73　Vera lectured at the night school
on composition. Bookish youth
came to the couple
for advice. Snow came, coats were made
and mended. Then spring, endless muddy roads.

74　Thick summer air badgers the horizon,
but there was indeed a town
made by hand, still, coming closer.
Progress begins in the unification of communities.

75　Another year and the war was over.
Some returned, most stayed.
Tomaz and Vera built a balloon house
cut from catalogue patterns memorized by a friend
in a prime lot gifted by committee.
Done, they sat in their back yard and watched
their river, hundreds of miles
from their old home.

76　A surprise.
Figures in black rising
from the water become the children they'd taught,
now young men and women.
Sets and props in a waterproof bag unpacked
became a stage.
The world at dusk transformed by lantern and torchlight.
A play to prepare the loved ones for sleep.

77   The rest of town arrived with chairs,
     a secret kept for free admission.
     A sudden fanfare, tuneless and bold,
     then quiet, and a lion appeared and spoke.

          Welcome to our happy few.
          Our town attained without gold
          or chain in retreat
          from an insane world.
          Light continues
          in the romance
          of breath and tree.

78   Our story is a story
          if a story is a meal;
          endless time bound
          in laughter sealed by friendship
          and the chance of love.

     The lion leaned into the last line
     with a pained look meant for a lover in the wings.
     A look seen by all. Giggles backstage.

79   As the moon rises
          you will see life
          reflected in company.
          What we call a constellation
          is a shape
          minds have made locating
          others out of darkness.
          These two we gather for,

Vera and Tomaz,
have mapped their love
onto us. We map
this love for you.

80 And there they were
on stage,
younger, setting table
for friends they would
never see again.
Popular music from
a radio in the corner,
the smell of salted garlic
and onion in oil coming
into the audience.

81 The soldiers had, of course,
found Vera's book. Healing
on a bumpy cart,
they'd read and re-read
her masterpiece, afraid every day
she'd find out and take it,
to worry over flaws
only she could see.

82 Because the book was encrusted
with Vera's many lives,
and because the young intellectuals
were also dancers, actors, singers,
philosophers or priests,

workers or farmers,

or simply a member of a family, arguments

about the book's adaptation

were long and passionate,

but always full of joy.

Out of one well-loved thing

the many find a love

accessible by all,

but newly shaped by one.

83   At last a consensus. Plot

would be transformed into character.

Each arc of Vera's novel—her fictionalized life,

her fantasies, her farces—was taken by an actor

and made into a person to be played. Some

were obviously real, as real as a memory;

others less so, though the embodiment

was no less potent as structure

representing existence beyond

the limits of physics and chemistry and math

as they appear before the mind

extends itself.

84   There they were,

lit by gas, recognizable

by all who

read the book

and all who

never read

but write

the world
to be read
by all.

85 Only the ark could contain more life.
In the dusk of the play's moment,
all other theater and poetry, useless.

86 What remains is a series of theatrical images,
flickering between symbol and object,
that resolve in the abstract
space of understanding:
the squid gathers water to swim.

87 Vera aged into complication
and so did these images.
Theater and architecture became
sculpture and painting.
The age of counterpoint
measured in the difference
between Cage and Bach:
actors describing birds
occupying discrete space
together without competition
and the all
of the earthly chorus without sense
of an other.

88 What comes after
speech divorced from movement?

Vera saw polyvalency
as historical; neither
did she find herself
through the mob nor
did she refuse progress
by re-centering the self
in relation to any part of it.

89   Instead of politics, ethics.
Instead of attention, judgment.
Instead of life, art.

90   All soldiers will become actors.

91   New war makes new ritual.
Gods birthed sexless
out of all sexes thighs.

92   The production overflowed.
Actors cooked onstage, then
brought brioche filled with meat and cheese
into the audience. Dialogue
was indistinguishable from delight.

93   The stage became a table.
Vera and Tomaz, together at the end,
welcomed each actor in turn,
thanked them, and with small discussion,
blessed them.

94 Food became dance,
    dance became small groups
    of light discussion, drinking.

95 The party was ending.
    Chairs stacked. Rubbish
    swept into an overfull bin.
    One bulb above,
    the moon.

96 Slow dispersion, but one
    last dance in silence
    for Vera and Tomaz.

97 Walking, holding hands,
    someone calls out to them
    from the darkness.

98 "But who was the silent girl on stage,
    pale, dressed in black?"

99 The lovers looked at each other
    and said—who else—
    "Elaine."

SANTA FE, 2018–2020

DEVIN KING is the
author of *There Three* and
The Grand Complication. Until
recently, he was the poetry editor
for The Green Lantern Press.
He lives in Oxford, UK, where he
is at work on a biography
of Ronald Johnson.

SELECTED BACKLIST